Under the Sea
Sea Otters

by Jody Sullivan Rake

Consulting Editor: Gail Saunders-Smith, PhD

Consultant: Deborah Nuzzolo, Education Manager
SeaWorld, San Diego, California

Capstone
press®

Mankato, Minnesota

Pebble Plus is published by Capstone Press,
151 Good Counsel Drive, P.O. Box 669, Mankato, Minnesota 56002.
www.capstonepress.com

1 2 3 4 5 6 12 11 10 09 08 07

Library of Congress Cataloging-in-Publication Data
Rake, Jody Sullivan.
    Sea otters / by Jody Sullivan Rake.
    p. cm.—(Pebble plus. Under the sea)
    Summary: "Simple text and photographs describe sea otters, their body parts, and what
they do"—Provided by publisher.
    Includes bibliographical references and index.
    ISBN-13: 978-1-4296-0034-7 (hardcover)
    ISBN-10: 1-4296-0034-9 (hardcover)
    1. Sea otter—Juvenile literature. I. Title.
QL737.C25.E35 2008
599.769'5—dc22   2006102228

Editorial Credits
Mari Schuh, editor; Juliette Peters, set designer; Kim Brown, book designer; Charlene Deyle, photo researcher

Photo Credits
© Susan Thomas/susanthomasphotos.com, 1
Corbis/Brandon D. Cole, 10–11; Joel W. Rogers, 20–21; Jonathan Blair, 6–7
Minden Pictures/Norbert Wu, 13, 14–15; Tim Fitzharris, 8–9
Peter Arnold/Malcolm Schuyl, cover; Thomas D. Mangelsen, 18–19
Seapics/Jane Vargas, 5
Tom & Pat Leeson, 16–17

Note to Parents and Teachers

The Under the Sea set supports national science standards related to the diversity
and unity of life. This book describes and illustrates sea otters. The images support
early readers in understanding the text. The repetition of words and phrases helps early
readers learn new words. This book also introduces early readers to subject-specific
vocabulary words, which are defined in the Glossary section. Early readers may need
assistance to read some words and to use the Table of Contents, Glossary, Read More,
Internet Sites, and Index sections of the book.

Table of Contents

What Are Sea Otters?. 4

Body Parts. 8

What Sea Otters Do 12

Under the Sea. 20

Glossary 22

Read More 23

Internet Sites. 23

Index .24

What Are Sea Otters?

Sea otters are sea mammals.

They live in shallow water

near rocky shores.

Sea otters have

long bodies.

They are about

the size of a big dog.

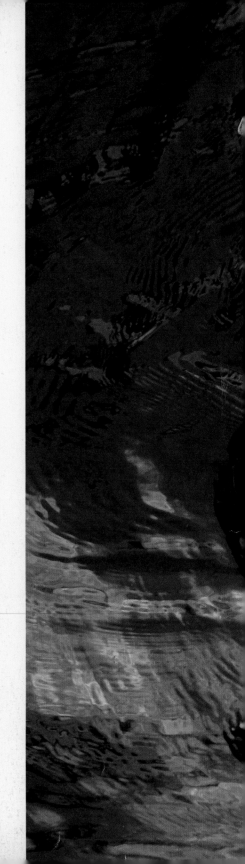

Body Parts

Soft, thick fur keeps
sea otters warm and dry.

Webbed feet

help sea otters

swim and dive.

What Sea Otters Do

Sea otters dive

to the ocean floor

to get prey.

Sea otters eat while
floating on their backs.
They eat lots of crabs,
clams, and sea urchins.

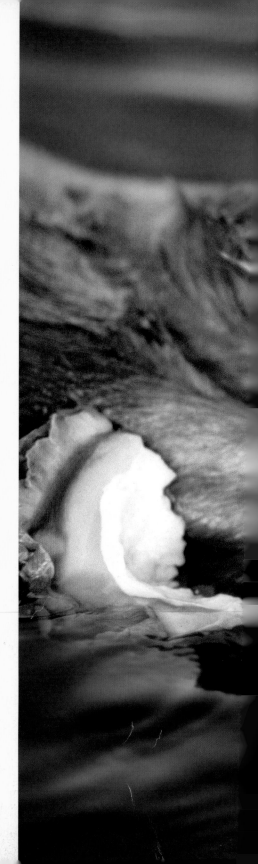

Sea otters groom
themselves often.
They clean and fluff
their fur.

Sea otters sleep in the water.
They wrap themselves
in seaweed to keep from
floating away.

Under the Sea

Sea otters

swim and dive

in the sea.

Glossary

dive—to swim down toward the bottom of a lake or ocean

groom—to clean; sea otters clean themselves so their fur can keep them warm and dry; dirty hair does not keep sea otters warm.

mammal—a warm-blooded animal that breathes air; mammals have hair or fur; female mammals feed milk to their young.

prey—an animal hunted by another animal for food

seaweed—a plant that grows underwater; sea otters often sleep in a kind of seaweed called kelp.

shallow—not deep

webbed feet—feet that have skin between the toes; webbed feet help sea otters swim fast.

Read More

Kendell, Patricia. *Sea Otters.* In the Wild. Chicago: Raintree, 2004.

Morris, Ting. *Otter.* Small Furry Animals. Mankato, Minn.: Smart Apple Media, 2006.

Pingry, Patricia A. *Baby Sea Otter.* SeaWorld Library. Nashville, Tenn.: CandyCane Press, 2006.

Internet Sites

FactHound offers a safe, fun way to find Internet sites related to this book. All of the sites on FactHound have been researched by our staff.

Here's how:

1. Visit *www.facthound.com*

2. Choose your grade level.

3. Type in this book ID **1429600349** for age-appropriate sites. You may also browse subjects by clicking on letters, or by clicking on pictures and words.

4. Click on the **Fetch It** button.

FactHound will fetch the best sites for you!

Index

bodies, 6

cleaning, 16

diving, 10, 12, 20

eating, 14

floating, 14, 18

fur, 8, 16

grooming, 16

mammals, 4

ocean floor, 12

prey, 12

seaweed, 18

shores, 4

size, 6

sleeping, 18

swimming, 10, 20

webbed feet, 10

Word Count: 106
Grade: 1
Early-Intervention Level: 14